Also by Mike Barnes

POETRY

Calm Jazz Sea
(Brick, 1996)

SHORT FICTION

Aquarium
(Porcupine's Quill, 1999)

Contrary Angel
(Porcupine's Quill, 2004)

NOVELS

The Syllabus
(Porcupine's Quill, 2002)

Catalogue Raisonné
(Biblioasis, 2005)

A THAW FORETOLD

Mike Barnes

a thaw FORETOLD

POEMS

BIBLIOASIS

FIRST EDITION

Library and Archives Canada Cataloguing in Publication

Barnes, Mike, 1955–
A thaw foretold / Mike Barnes.

Poems.
1-897231-19-9

I. Title.
PS8553.A7633C37 2005   C811'.54   C2006-901948-7

Edited by ERIC ORMSBY

We acknowledge the support of the Canada Council
for the Arts for our publishing program.

PRINTED AND BOUND IN CANADA

for Heather

Contents

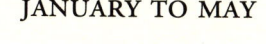

JANUARY TO MAY

January

Last night the pipes froze again
and we dreamed in tandem of a death.
You said it happened in a car crash
and in my dream it was cancer.
A fiery smash, a slow riddling —
over takeout coffee and fruit salad
the difference seemed too innocent to split.
A splitting of hairs beside the silence
in the pipes and the silent way our minds
roiled in black together, our warm hips touching.
You held my arm for a moment
as we kissed, and asked me to be careful.
Your face is what I know now as I ease
into traffic, your lips against this melting.

Danaë

This cloud of bright shards
falls to your eager soft ears:

God that first glimpse of blue
through the trees. Dad,
mopping his pink forehead at the end
of a long portage. I
set the canoe in the tall grass by the shore
and sat beside him on a warm rock, gasping.

Taking tennis lessons, the first thing
that goes is your old game. So,
stressed Dr. B, there is a phase
of progress that consists
in having no game, no game at all.
This must be endured.
As nightmares must, as filling tubs?
Just so, his steepled fingers.

I'm only a prick on the
surface. Under that I'm a nice guy.
Of course under that . . .

There was no note.
And you said, disputing
the common tongue, you can't
call that vengeance, spite. Don't let's
go too easy on ourselves. They
also omit who mean to write,
who plan to keep talking. (Their end
in their eyes is not their end
in yours, you planned to say, but broke
off, embarrassed by the hush.) —

You in the pregnant tomb
cannot be shamed by a god's lust.

Cable

I glimpsed the depths I knew I'd plunge
and with an oxy-
acetylene torch unseal the slimed vaults lodged there.

Fate is an oldfashioned word, you murmured.
And that unbelief, and more the wiry strands of hair
scratching a lost doubloon below one hanging gull

are what I cling to in this lidless dark and delving.

Moleskine

Let me help you with your tunnelling, she said.
There is a store. An art store packed with stuff,
and staffed by decent people that you know
(you met them at that pub in December);
you could come in near closing time, when it's quiet,
and check out these great new notebooks they've got —
soft as wallets, but firm inside, with a clean-opening
spine, and a slim black band to close it up, elasticized
like a garter. Van Gogh had one and swore by it.

We could go for sushi afterward, she said
before she left. And were I not so nearly dumb
with coping and companion shame (this now
only by way of apology and trust) I might explain
how snout and scrabbling feet do not bump up against,
much less push through, the friable grains of days,
but go, somehow, right past them. Past.

Sprawl

Is there time for a small poem just now,
amid the numb or frenzied packing, the voices sounding
last-call? If so, here's one. You and I
speeding down off the Barrie snow plains
back to Toronto, cresting one of those long familiar hills
you said, "The sprawl," and then I saw it:
a vast fretwork of lights shimmering
to the horizon, unfurling
an umbrella of glow in miles of milky haze.
A city. Our city. It spelled us
with its intricacy, blithe power and extent,
and to think, we gushed in our speeding
black capsule down again, not even the smallest of the gleams
not planned, manufactured, installed and kept lit
by someone. We drove under that aura,
blinking up at it like mice at the Milky Way,
but Russian-dolled inside our awe
was the fact that "the sprawl", the phrase itself,
came from a novel we'd both read and loved.
                    That, too,
invoked a galaxy behind the rock, a sprawl inside the sprawl.

Storm

River picture of him on a friend's photo shelf,
holding a skinny pike. Johnson 20, choppy bay behind.
My trophy! Love — in small neat script on the back.

(How can it not say more? The question gets asked.
But (speculating here) if a life's lived in time, its record is too,
and the caption fits the moment which was still — just — before.)

Not five minutes past that shutter click, he and the one
behind the lens, whom he still won't confine
in a name beyond *she*, stood drenched and gaping on a slope of

rain-slicked rock, beside a channel gone abruptly still
except for the sizzle of pelting drops — so hard
they felt like hail — sequestering them in straight white sheets;

behind that veil, black cliffs shook with a roar
that rolled and rumbled and crashed
inside a giant funnel of stone, a

bowling ball stumbling in a circular gutter, or
(one of them said) a huge roulette wheel churning, with them
at the bottom, stopped. *No warning — it just blew up.*

(*Weather can turn on a dime*, he'll say.
Brusquely, so you won't add *Life, too* or think he meant it.
He married, found a job, has children and grandchildren.)

You want to extend the story. Freeze-frame
one missing bit and enlarge it. When the cobalt
and white trees began branching everywhere, perverse

bleached veins that pulsed a moment in amber glare,
mightn't there have been some seconds
when they looked at each other not with fright but thrill

at the rain's battering skin, the racket, and forked air?
You can't tell. There is his colourful description
(unstinting but invariable) and then the news accounts.

(*Weather can change that fast if you're out in it.*
And once, with a tired smile: *That little snake was gone
in a flash. I hope he found some thick, thick weeds.*)

The Purple Finch

Parlous to seek signs
in doggerel times.

This raspberry head
flicking side-eyed

gleams into this room
may just have come

to warm its face
near a flash of glass

(though along the sill
there is ice still).

Aún aprendo

A mentor? Immediate.
Goya's small chalk drawing, done at eighty-
something, of a stooped, bearded, ancient
man, making his way with the aid of two canes
— "god-on-sticks" the English critic called him.
White highlights on his forward thigh
declare him keeping just ahead
of the massed black shadow scrawled behind.
The caption: *Aún aprendo.*
"I'm still learning."

        (That plus
the slim-hipped girl who just rubbed
boyfriend's face with snow, her red cheeks
tipped to a graphite sky, laughing.)

Touched

Past the brute but already
receding marvel of Burnt Island,
aspen tips poking through the char,
a more mysterious circle of desolation:
smack in the middle of normal woods
not far from the river where
we'd beached for some reason,
this criss-cross of downed trees,
some with their leaves still on,
green and fluttering. It was a scene
of random chaos to me, the more dire
for being uncaused (and so local
and so small): no swamp
to drown roots, no sign of loggers' roads,
ordinary-looking woods beyond,
ordinary woods on our return
(cool trunks slapped just to be sure).

We zipped up (that was it)
and Dad, more rarely
and so more memorably telepathic
than Mom, observed, "A storm passed through."
No glance back at me, his trademark
curse and crash through foreign bush begun.

But perhaps he sensed I couldn't let it go,
or was reckoning it himself, for he
added in a musing tone, our motor idling now,
"It just touched down." And that was it.
No amount of cold spray gunnelled back
could quench the thought of storm
as sprite. Storm
as eagle with fixed talons and crazed dive,
snatching the rightways course of green up into sky.

Meshaw Falls

If you stand on a bridge in a picture
I can see you. Hold you

by a thumbtack pressed in crumbling drywall,
your hair more unruly

than ever in that breeze,
your sun hat shadowing a questing smile,

a smile to one you trust.
Some said, and doubtless more thought, we could not

meet on any such bridge,
for any such summer.

But we crossed the span easily, and though now
I glimpse the waterfall's

white churn spill down into
a quiet bay beside an unused structure

I will hold this vision of you as you
for as long as wind and planking will allow.

Acolyte

And if you know there's a fire,
or suspect there may be,
and build a cabin of sticks
and blow in air, and *are* warmed,
though not by flames, not actually,
but by the glow of the tricks
your busy hands performed,
this welter of sparks and smoke in the air?

We call that a prayer for prayer.

The Ice Chisel

Two-thirds of a man's
height, the instrument

makes a rough golden
mean with the thigh-high frozen

mound blocking the driveway
(if "golden" can apply

to this shelf of stone
neglect — "mean" certainly can).

The science of fracture
is not to pit your

weight but to add to the blade,
let the long sharp spade

head find the angle
willing to crack. *I'll*

bet that feels good says
a passerby as

you hoist some freed chunks on
a shovel, hurl them down

the air to crash and
splinter where they land.

For answer let iron
rust a moment in sun,

speak (in a brittle code)
of a thaw long foretold.

The Watcher

First to last you had to watch it all.
More than anyone else, more than doctors
or nurses doing their jobs, more than I,
transfixed on a bed or gurney, catching
stray glimpses of a sick ghost in chrome,
you had to witness what was happening
in slow erosions or midnight blasts
that left craters and interminable winters.
Some watching was your lot as a mother
but the constancy of it was yours. Each
day riding the bus downtown alone,
no weekends off. Cookies, muffins
for the staff and other incarcerants
too sick to nibble. What I pluck out
from long amnesias are your scuffed white
Adidas — you who loved to dress up
(I had watched you as a child) in silk
nylons and high, litigious black heels.
But this was a race now, or perhaps
a muddy plod. Your hair careless
(the bus coming!), your ski jacket stained.
Your voice conquering an amiable nature
to scream, No! You do something! Now!
Two years. And then the promise:
There'll be more. More random, perhaps
even more severe. I can't unburn
those sad terrors from your eyes
but only wash them a little with these lines,
as once, with infinite faith, you waited to wash mine.

Abdication

Despair, you have held sway with me too long:
joint monarchs of a kingdom of cold light
together we've stoppered joy, poured what might
have been good wine down to the dregs of wrong.
How many holidays have we combined
to sow sad ruin, black seeds in mists of grey
harvesting this weekday stubble of day
stumbling into day like Bruegel's pitching blind?
You trained me as a prince in loathsome arts:
grim inwardness, outfacing cheer, horror
that outfaceted a fly's eye in sun.
Though there's no dissevering such welded hearts,
though nothing can slake the bloodless thirst for
loss that is you, know this: *our* rule is done.

The Return

Solid the four-foot-thick river ice on our way
across. Sunlight filling your boot treads with pale lemon.

Solid too on our return until the moment
you dropped through by a dock buried ten feet from shore.

Ginger ale and ice cubes tinkled round your floundering.

Level your mind always, thoughts fused, in a crisis.
Stay back, you rasped, *stay back*, to my panicked runs

in at the widening hole, and when you walrused out
to gasp on shore: *I think we'll make it. Hurry, though.*

The cabin smoke curling a boy's short run away.
But your limbs now going stiff, robotic, dream-like, slow,

alien as a baby's birthed at forty below.

Redux

A woman with a lizard mask made up
of folded white sheets locks eyes in Frankfurt.

Two men play chess from towers directing
other men to make their keg-sized pieces

clash on a checked lawn. Beer foams in glasses.
The chessmen reappear without masters

and grown ten feet tall in Frogner Park, Oslo:
a national monument fêting the

"human family" in granite — what to do
except run? Grey stone, grey sky, grey faces.

Then Technicolor blooms, thuggishly lush,
of Liz Taylor and Rock Hudson, *Giant*

faces overspilling the tablecloth marquee.
Behind the lobby grille, swathed in shadow,

the lizard one removes her bandages
slowly: Lisbet you kissed at three in a

sandbox, blonde face turned, parents snapping.

Broke

The money's gone
the cash is spent

nothing I own
that isn't lent.

What have I done
in times like these

in times of stone
no birds no bees?

Nothing to do
but take a walk

make yourself go
around the block.

The nearest bar
is the oldest stop

cadge a jar
of whatever's on tap.

Unkenning

What is this thing
breaking in you again?

White spilling veils,
sun cupped in palm —

the conceit is a shell
plucked from a sonnet,

its theft but a name
for milk-flour yearning

with the oven this hot,
so close to burning.

Claws

Lift the rock.
(Just ease it back.)

See the shelled creature,
copper-bluish-green

freeze itself in time
assaying the changed light

then scoot
back with a brisk

down-snap
of articulated tail.

Tiny whirlpool where
it was, rising.

Reared back against
the dark-sustaining

algae-furred ledge,
antennae bristling

small serrated claws
open to all visitors.

Shh, a finger
next to chapped lips

says, the head flick
back at the martini

sippers on the deck.
They don't know they're here.

Judgement

Ani in the afterworld
works.

Tills soil, scatters seed,
harvests and threshes grain.

Blue canals
enclose his fields,
enfold him in flowing water.

Labourlessly
affluent in life,
his soul, weighed

by the balance
of his heart
against Maat's feather

(scales adjusted
by Anubis, results
recorded by Thoth)

has been granted
the papyrus play
the granite solace

of toil.

Ghost World

Once I sang from a cage
  of flesh, sweetly burning;
now I dress in the dark
of these bones, slipping past locks
  with a knock and murmur of rhyme.

The night I feared
as empty and teeming
  swells deep with
  shadowed forms. Deals
get struck between skin, moon and rain.

Sheer disbelief is the passage across,
hidden in this discovery:
  sun comes up
  and we are still here, flickering,
stable as dust in a gust of orange.

War was constant:
  I see that now. Enemies
surrounded me or I rushed to meet them:
implacable, stronger,
  I bless the weapons that bought

this converse and feel remorse,
  pungent but fleeting
as a dream of wrong, for each hour
  bound in numb fierce
combat, never ardent to find this seeking.

Garbage Day

A mistake has been made.
A larger truck or a more zealous
crew has taken it all away.
The houses stand clean-limbed and tall,
solid as their builders envisioned.
Open or closed their curtains
admit the light's glad ferocity,
scouring and annealing each particular.
The marmelade cat strangely
chinning itself on the crossbar
of the glinting mesh fence,
the line of tattered grey snow
self-disposing in the shadow
of the shed. A snapped shingle.
Where did the strength or
vision come from to remove it all
this time? The clutter, the detritus,
the festinating whims and thoughts,
so human, that make time a stumble
down a barely glimpsed corridor.
A metronome will pace this day,
its lone tocking that of clarity.

K

The brain that wakes in the night
speaks with a battering lucidity:
*Swallow all the pills and she can
use the money to get a nice place.*

And if you don't and she doesn't
— if (in other words) yesterday and tomorrow?
But the voice admits no before and after,
no cause and effect linking arms:

it startles when the necklace drops, a warm
clattering, and tracks the faceted clarity
of a gemstone glinting in the black
of a corner, a pearl's milk in the dust.

If potassium needed a voice
it might speak like this:
K, that strangest of elements you met
inside the brick house on the hill,

stolid in oil, a fatty lump drifting
ponderously — a metal, really? — that can be
cut like butter with a knife — the intense
gleam of a silver-white face shining

for a second then crusting over in black,
renegades in the air flocking to its
perverse volatility, its avidity to combine.
Burn under water with an arc welder's spitting,
                              violet flame.

Cures can be new but the best are oldest.
The softly patting hand, the glass of warm milk.
Infant soothing first, then questions for the adult
that must talk: *What is it like?*

Like? Like. Like. *Try this.* It is like
waking to spare birdsong on a deserted beach
— *like Crusoe, then?* — No, yes, but with no memory
of getting there, no voyage behind or

ahead, no sense utterly of coming from
or going to, only this noon of marvels which do not,
disarmingly, shock. Tirelessly sifting
the hot sparking crystals, pacing the shoreline

round to confirm its emptiness: lime-grey surf
slurping the pebbles, flickers of the no-longer-
singing birds in the steep forest, scarlet flames.
It is perhaps first when day fails to end,

no natural subsidence into dusk, that you infer
something super- or trans-tropical at work
and conjure memories you can hardly trust,
though you must, of the trip over water:

engine throb, the pleasing reek of brine and oil,
the other passengers, some fractious,
some strangers, some your friends —
the precocious little girl who tossed a plastic

party favour over the stern and was
lectured by "green" parents — that was a laugh,
wasn't it? the tiny pink in the vast bubbling wake;
and there was reason too, compelling logic

for this sojourn in fierce slanted light
— recollections of the argument seem sound
or at least forceful — and a promise made
to return, pick up, and take away. That

is when night will fall as it should, hugs
and kisses back, and stories to tell
of a diverging ocean. Potassium will again
be as it is, a member of the family of alkali

metals, neighbour of sodium and calcium,
and K, no freak, will find
his place in the pages
of a book by a dark-eyed Czech.

Fledgling

When did you stop
stooping to pick up
a green and purple feather
shining by the curb?

One swoop and pluck
— remember? — and with
pin or tape or glue
such a treasure
would complete a letter
or adorn a gift,
preserve a poem or passage,
make fledgling a
mirror frame or window sill.

To pass by now
with just a glance of interest
reveals how many
declensions you've mastered
in the grammar of neglect.

Scraps interred
in cotton batting caskets,
pebbles glinting
in clear pill bottle water,
acorns, ribbons, shells,
chestnuts polished unto shrivelling —

Oh, you can re-learn
perhaps, but not in the same classroom.
When you return
after your errands, an oval
shard of someone's plastic shades
has replaced it cunningly

catching the light
in a similar way.

Nocturne

Never mind the windows
flooding with almond light

the crocuses just below
bruising purple, yellow, green

Wrapped in an afghan
knit by fingers nearly bone

admit the Messenger of nerves:
April 5. 5 p.m. Day is done.

The Unnamed

I cannot celebrate
— not privately —
your arrival in this zone.

There is no personal
here. You are ground
without figure. Number, not miracle.

I feel no less alone
— nor more — for all
that you twist my gut

with that acid of expectancy
recalled from Christmases —
the flattish prickling *what?*

when joy not nested
in toys, fun, food
declined to swoop on schedule

though it might fall
after all, unasked-
for, with a private face

to slash the heart
full, not
in the prepared rooms

but, lance-like, in corridors.

"Bloomsbury"

My head's seen better days —
                              a tribute to last night!
          and the reeling, "Roman-style" time we had.

My stomach's iffy too —
                    yet I still inhale
                    deeply from the vase
                    of flowers and the unstoppered wine
                        friends left behind

      preferring to gag
      on a surfeit of celebration

than to return — too soon —
to the usual diet of prudence and strangers.

Honey Locust

Sneak into the celebration tonight
to watch her mingle with the crowd.
What for? Not to confirm
you don't belong, your lack of proper attire
only the most obvious of the reasons why.
She doesn't belong either: that look
you shared this morning as she dressed
in her "disguise" of heels, gelled hair, black
blouse and a coat you've never seen before
said, on her part, *What a laugh*
and *Do I pass?* The second part's the laugh.
She'll easily be the lustre of that room,
inciting admiring and envious looks, and,
in corners, gossip about *Who is she? Who?*
But you don't need to witness that again.
You've nothing against the people there
and you know they'll never tempt her away —
in private, at least, admit your lack of jealousy.
So why, then? Why the recurring fantasy
of yourself peering from the margins
like some rat-man out of Dostoyevsky, Hamsun, Gogol?
The answer's in the pale yellow buds of the
honey locust just outside the window, in
the thick veins of the hand holding open this notebook:
you're still here. And to believe
that takes this seeping of crazed rains.

River

It makes for an inverted epilogue,
when, to a spectral prelude,
    a skeletal start,
the busy, seeking meat gets tacked.

    No more wandering
in mists that glide and wind, thickening
round milky shine. Instead, to clutch
solid fruit, other flesh, risk too-much

after the scrimp-marsh of not-enough.
    Who said it was tough
to cope with impedimenta or
strife? The cot in the corridor,

the grime-rife pane, the veins that slept
and the room that sparked: these precepts
packed your craft to pole over death
    across to life.

AUGUST TO JANUARY

First Stab

Something is off in you, she said,
and, happy it wasn't *she* half-dead,
she based her kisses on it.
Body over mind responded
(at seventeen no great contest)
and from Valentine's till harvest
we flew to the lust part faster
when we realized what a vaster
illness, like mental leprosy,
was rotting the limbs and lips we
could still unironically call blessed
as hotly they, as we, caressed.
A better one could cure this stuff,
whispered a voice, dismissing love.

Shapes

Eye of blue
in a bank of cloud

holding its own
in a wind that veered,

narrowed down
to a slit bestowed

just as a new
lens opened and peered.

Morning Glories

Morning glories climbed as never before
the summer before his death.
Muting colours of pale sunrise
— lavender, rose-pink, washed blue and white —
they climbed out of the cracked dry dirt
in the pots neglected on the balcony.
Up the jammed stakes and across
the black floral curlicues of wrought iron
they spread with almost-wild
profusion, with magical abandon.
Their rate of shrivelling was an astonishment,
too — one crisp blare of colour
whose first echo was crimped petals,
then a drooping, then a withered fallen sack.
And I remember, too, the wet,
sticky wonder of their strenuous tendrils,
like the wet tiny fingers of fetuses
budding and lengthening and groping for light.
Regardless of outer colour, each trumpet
funnelled to a core of ethereal white,
so delicate it seemed to merge with air,
almost vanishing in a corridor
from music to its shadowed source.
                    Sometimes,
on those hot still August afternoons,
the spade-shaped leaves trembled in no breeze,
tensed to renew their breathless digging in air.

Dread

Why write a poem — or read one —
if its lines could
not breathe in your ears?

Why watch a wave
catch on a rock
exactly like a duck splashing off

if not to turn
and see the image
paralleled in your eyes, true?

Why take a step?
Why draw breath?

Singular life can be reclaimed.
Perhaps. In some cases, yes.
But the truly grafted tree
will not be split.
It flourishes or dies as one.

Only to stay true,
the moment of recall:
to turn and say
to dark, "I'm coming too."

Yorick

A month after moving, one last bag,
the small black vinyl one, still
loitered in the car. Contents:
the top half of an animal's skull
(species never known) and, since
it hadn't been worn in years,
a green velvet hat to cushion it.
Would that stand jostling with this bottle
of gin? Under a stifling hatchback
thirst and caution sang a short duet.
Guarded well from concrete knocks, once
upstairs, the bag revealed a capful
of white dust scented with junipers.

Eagles

No teeter of black wings,
vile wobble against the sun,
or the miserly
shrunken head, blood-red
blot to hide a beak in.

No eagles here.
On this point the guidebook is firm.
But what carrion-eater
ever rode the air
with such majestic calm,

or, circling, found
another to intersect
with in such companionable-looking
                              loops?

No. Even if all the facts
said "turkey vulture", and all logic too,
that is not what we saw
that day in Wahnapitei Bay, not
what we had, or what we briefly knew.

Song

Ask for more and you might get squat.
Ask for it all
and the collection plate
you think you control
is sure to shrink
to a cracked saucer, and tilt as well

and your hoard of heaped riches
— of marbles, dollars, friends,
and love, and art gained slowly,
and the unanointed time
you prize above all: windows
and walks between crocus and snow
and bud again, blood-ample seconds in the sun —

will jostle obscenely
in a kind of lifeboat brawl,
then slide off and crash
on some unthinkable floor.

Bold Street

Black jolt of fur,
a spasming leg —
between them the slur
of white painted steel,
the driver agog
in the grip of the wheel.

Church

Have you paid your tithe today?
The nod to the neighbour
who never nods back,
the application for funds
to be sat on a year
then shat back as goose egg

over *Project unclear.*
Other payments come due
to the civilized state:
the grins over gravy
swabbing the family plate,
mothballing demurs

about crap called sublime,
then sitting *stumm*
when the brilliant's called dumb.
Balls to all that.
You're not nailed to the pew.
Absolutely true — and the biggest tithe too.

Chasing Grace

A day without hurry comes closest to God,
I heard as a sinner must hear talk of good.
Whenever from childhood I've found myself still,
my senses switched on, my will in neutral,
a teeming begins, a swarming from hives,
centrifugal *Go now!*s and clock hands and eyes;
among vagrant feelings, this one persists:
a parentless squirming of *can't-do-but-must.*
Traditional cures — Buddha, sex, alcohol —
could slow but not stop the mechanical steal
of nothing from something, echo from yell
clamouring to kick-start what silence might stall.
Haste comes of the devil, the adage ended —
time's swiftest skills are on evil dependent.

Ward Love

Shadowless shade,
your image
haunts me purely.

In no amnesia
yet dreamed
can I annul

the slimed vows
you hoard, eelgrass
plighting our troth,

or clasp the locks
long rusted off
the boxes lost mid-crossing.

You proffer visions
lush with gloom:
the smog eyes of warders

bent on salvage,
asphalted meadows
heaped with fluorescent

trash, smashed cabinets,
pinkish slabs, chrome spokes
gridlocked in glass.

Rank warpings of air
prefigured and survived
your midnight floats across,

your bare feet fleet
over clammy tiles,
illegible ink

of hair and eyes,
the pale glimmerings
of nightgown and face

insubstantially sad,
what you whispered
unforgotten as wind

trying the cracked frame.
Marry me . . . marry . . .
and then the ritual

lifting of your soiled
shift slowly,
offering starved breasts

razored and glowing.
Red shiny milk
for the ones with bones . . .

And the darkness
we spelled then
still pronounces us home.

Swimmers

A middleaged man and a young man with a beard
(lover or son? gets conjectured after they leave):
the younger lurches, flailing his limbs, emits high yelps
while his companion patiently marshals him
through shave, shower, shallow-end paddle, towel, dress,
                                        Sprite.

Another pair are of an age and quieter,
but the same ties of tender dependence bind them:
the sighted one keeps his hand on his friend's elbow,
steering his bland white eyes until he smells the chlorine.
While he floats near the ladder the guide churns twelve
                                        lengths.

Sometimes these four seem the sole swimmers in the pool,
the rest of us just bathers, death-wranglers, lounge acts,
                                        seals.

Swamp Elegy

May lush green
fronds and stark
yellow flowers decorate
the pool where
Tynan's friends tie
him to stones.

Rain

Who would call this
the first winter rain
which is not cold, which is not freezing?

It yet persuades
by a power of change,
by forces that shift beyond their keeping.

Clouds split wide
and spill torrents down,
then trail to filmy, world-blearing curtains;

tricklings now,
quiverings in black,
give way to the pause of a grey-faced mountain.

Old age, I see,
is such a rain;
though not yet cold, though not yet freezing

it will proceed
by a power of change
and faces that shift beyond their keeping.

Ox Bay

Geese honked in the night,
thickening darkness with hoarse calls,
and we, eating by candlelight,
seemed to see beyond the cabin's walls
their wings outstretched,
the webbed feet lowered,
feeling for water after the long day's flight.

Though we stared at black, and sidelong
    at each other,
just the rough, rich, urgent sounds
could bring feathers and long necks,
    a wave-rocked
gabble and paddle into our minds.

Now geese honk by day,
curt cries distinct in this white room,
and though I jump out of the chair,
the arrowing vee with changing leaders
is nowhere in the sky.
                Through windows that are
wide and polished, what I see feels like blindness:
a mobile shining grey, pale leaves quaking,
with dottings of jets like pepper grains floating —
hissing, imageless. The calls do not resume.

Gardener

Is this then strategy? To gain some purview
unattainable by the teenage knight
pinning on isolate square his mastery?
Or is that to configure threadbare as new,
picture as game a battle by twilight,
clip hedges in the garden of sorcery?

Cameo

Iron Age features — courage, strength, grace —
rounded, not softened, by irony's trace.

The Literate

Told at nine she could not read
(*low verbals* a baton
passed from mother to teachers
to Board psychometrist)
she answered the doctor, "I read."

She walks in books as in woods
or by lakes, parsing the season,
tasting its smells, spotting
the curious snail or mushroom
deep in a crack or oak's shade.

She reads with fingers, fleshing
airy symbol, face kiss-close
to the page, and when the letters
change places she goes with them,
at ease with senses turning.

In roomfuls of the literate
she sits aside, her book bag
wrong here though she can't say
why. Talk is dabbed with napkins.
She traces the lines on her plate.

Wires and Walls

The world ran on
where I left it;
I could tell
by the sounds
spare as birdsong
— memory or call —
that reached me
after long delay
through thickening walls,
down wires frayed.

Kindling

Against the clear October sky
leaves drift down to earth
haphazardly.
    Close by, across the
scarred pine table lacquered with sun,
Livia progresses on *A Desert Frost*,
its alien world gone arid
from the neglect of critical machines.
    Coffee smells of
time secured: like frying onions,
like vanilla, it brings back moments whole.
I return to reading *Phaedo* —
twenty years on I am still a little
bored, less convinced by Socrates'
reasoning and more moved by his farewell.
Dumbstruck by the soul, I am
cheered when anyone avers it.
    The clock tells me
it's time to prepare: as usual,
clinging to routines, unnerved by travel,
I've cut it fine.
    Still I must
shave carefully around a scar
and not nick myself yet again.
As a boy what I loved most
about leaf piles were the slivers of sky,
lancings of blue through the musty
crunch and sloughed skins, that might
have been some vestige, distant even then,
of peek-a-boo — the same awe, fright, delight,
piercing comfort.
    Today I feel calm,
as I note by the shamanistic slowness
with which I wash, brush, floss, lay out my clothes.
The sputter and splash of the shower's
warm drizzle, its hiss and liquid crackling

make me think of kindling
catching at various points and building;
                    so easily
does this image mingle with the general
unspooling I feel this autumn morning
that I wonder, a damp
patch pausing, at my own absence of alarm,
just this mindful dry peace spreading
and this unrushed readiness to go.

Stir

From inside this place
I can't see you well.

You survive behind walls
fraught with vague shimmers,

in echoless clangs
that might be your call.

Night upon night
your visit at noon

blots with black light
this dream in a room.

Our compact is firm
as a blade in a hole:

I don't say how you live,
you don't speak where I dwell.

Remembrance

Curled in a green chair
don't care to question
the grain that slants the air,

this sooty mist,
thread-bossed, close everywhere,
making angles of the most round.

Only turn in time to see
the house-sized bouquet
of quivering ashen leaves

beside the maculate
black branches huddled,
spindly in their ceremony,

blazon the extreme logic of loss,
its dogged deep descent
through the garden of knives,

the annealed dream of blood petals.

Album

If I could hold a pistol point to time,
would I return you to that beach, that day?
Your neck would still be straight and well,
no sign yet of its pillared bones
compacting into numbness, sharding into pain;
your bare feet set in slewing sand,
and the glistening on your face and arms
the dew of play, not therapy.
The man in shades beside you
would stay then, too — abandoning this frame
to give himself complete again
to beer and fish and chips, to driving in the car.
His share of us would be too green,
too tendrilled for the spacious barn
where columned light sifts shadows
into motes; and he would know
the darkening ripeness of our years
only as a tiller dreams a field:
unspoiled, ungatherable.

Anhedonia

Today you made a patient war
on boredom and despair —
or on something less
than these, or more:

anhedonia
a doctor called it once,
and the way he murmured it
impatiently, as if recalling
a bit of a pest

made you see a plain-
faced, plain-named woman
standing half in shadow,
half indifferently out,

meek-chinned, with dogged eyes:
she'd wait until you guessed
what had been done to her,
or hadn't, and by whom,

and when you, awkwardly,
tried to make it right,
she'd move off slowly,
still keeping you in sight.

Birthday

Time births the moment
in white glare —

past a weeping willow
in a suburb dead with sun —

a yellow tennis ball
crosses your path
on an August afternoon;
you hear it bounce
once, on the pavement,
see it whir
across the sidewalk
like a sly sun
spinning into grass;
for a moment it is all
that would escape,
shrinking and rushing
to do so...the cool green blades —

but look, it is simpler:
a boy waits
beyond the road, cross-
hatched by a wire fence,
his bat slung awkwardly —

only take one step
to clear the willow;

toss it to him,
underhand.

Genealogy

My forefather was a frightened man,
storm-sundered in the way of sand;
who turned himself into a fist,
then planned a table with his mind
to land upon with the hand he'd wished.

The world he could stand was smooth
and polished fine: more needful now,
and bold, than the hapless grid of truth
my youthful taunts had him scuttling on:
You can't stand curves or shadow.

This was the motto of a clan:
to simplify, always simplify;
encoding the actions of leaf and stem
down to a bulb in a cellar
meant, *I am stored against dark winter.*

Two types somehow summarized us all:
those who did too much and saw too little,
those who did too little and saw too much;
blind pharaohs blundering to a pyramid
and clairvoyant slaves without a reed.

And I can only lean a little from this line.
Der Apfel fällt nicht weit vom Baum.
Losing complexity like a genetic curse
I spin a little further than the rest
through swords of green, though still a frightened man.

Waste Spaces

Waste spaces, alleys, vacant lots,
dead streets deserted in the middle of the night:
these neglected, nowhere zones
have been to me what others say they find

in parks, fine houses, boulevards:
a stopping place for the caravan,
the trickling back in of spirit
after it has been depleted or misused.

I can speculate but not explain
why a discarded paper cup tossing on cracked asphalt
welcomes me and lifts me up
better than any crystal glass on polished sideboard.

In something dusty and long laid aside
there is a gleam of clarity and hope,
just as in the sparkling new a shroud
confounds, the film of being derelict and lost.

Seconds

"Too big in the shoulders, too small in the waist"
Dad used to joke as, one by one,
my brothers and I tried his old shirts on.
Growing bones soon gave him the lie,
time played his predictions false.
And now this last blue model I'm given to try
fits perfectly, squeezing across the chest.

Picking Up Steaks

The meat was where Dad
said it would be —
fridge freezer, Post-It note attached.
His directions always clear,
admirably succinct.
But you didn't expect
(why not?) the smells
of the shut-up house
to be so rich
after just two days,
a deepened marinade
of bodies, clothing, furniture
that you sniff warily,
conscious of its power.
The cool air does not
drift: it hangs,
still but for your passing.
Dim and granular
under the overhang,
the curtains pulled halfway,
like the deeply private
dusk beneath a mushroom,
shadowed from the sun.

Acknowledgements

My thanks to the editors of the following magazines in which these poems, sometimes in slightly different form, first appeared: *The New Quarterly*: "Meshaw Falls," "The Watcher," "Abdication," "Ghost World," "River," "First Stab," "Morning Glories," "Genealogy"; *Event*: "The Return"; *The Fiddlehead*: "Garbage Day"; *nthposition*: "Album," "Anhedonia"; *The Fieldstone Review*: "Sprawl."

I am grateful to the Canada Council for a grant which afforded me time to work on this manuscript.

Long before they saw publication, these poems benefited from the generous and thoughtful responses of two readers in particular: Heather Simcoe and Robyn Sarah. I am indebted to them both.

In editing this book, Eric Ormsby offered criticism that in its candour, sensitivity and insight proved most valuable. I thank him heartily.

Mike Barnes is the author of the novels *Catalogue Raisonné* and *The Syllabus*, and the short fiction collections *Aquarium* — winner of the 1999 Danuta Gleed Award for best first book of short fiction — and *Contrary Angel*. His first poetry collection, *Calm Jazz Sea*, was shortlisted for the Gerald Lampert Memorial Award. He lives in Toronto. (PHOTO: HEATHER R. SIMCOE)

A Thaw Foretold by Mike Barnes
Typeset in Adobe Garamond and Optima by Dennis Priebe
Printed, Smyth-sewn & bound by Gaspereau Press
Text: Rolland Zephyr Laid
Cover: Saint-Armand Handmade Paper
Printed in an edition of 400 copies

BIBLIOASIS
WINDSOR, ONTARIO